The Acropolis

Publishers: George A. Christopoulos, John C. Bastias
Managing Editor: Efi Karpodini — Dimitriadi
Translation: Harry Hionides
Special Photography: Spyros Tsavdaroglou, Mauro Pucciarelli

The Acropolis

MANOLIS ANDRONICOS

Professor of Archaeology at the University of Thessalonike

EKDOTIKE ATHENON S.A.
Athens 1990

ISBN 960-213-006-7

Copyright © 1980

by

EKDOTIKE ATHENON S.A.

1, Vissarionos Street

Athens 106 72, Greece

PRINTED AND BOUND IN GREECE

by

EKDOTIKE HELLADOS S.A.

An affiliated company

8, Philadelphias Street, Athens

THE ACROPOLIS AND THE MUSEUM

A HISTORY OF THE ATHENIAN ACROPOLIS

THE PREHISTORIC AGE

The sun-bathed plain of Athens extends in a semicircular sweep from Phaleron Bay to the foothills of the mountains in the hinterland of Attica. In its centre rises an imposing rock 156.2 metres above sea level, measuring 330 metres in length at the base, 270 metres at the summit, and slightly over 156 metres in width. This is the much-sung and much-praised Acropolis of Athens. The early inhabitants of the Neolithic Age built their crude dwellings in the confined space since it offered complete security and a safe refuge from enemies. All sides of the hill are precipitous and the only feasible approach is from the West. Moreover, a stream of clear sparkling water — a blessing to the early settlers — gushed from a crevice in the northwestern corner of the rock. This was to feed in later years the famous Klepsydra spring. In all probability the inhabitants of the Acropolis worshipped their benevolent god of water and the magnanimous deity who had blessed them with the olive-clad plain and the security of the natural citadel, the Acropolis, the name of which signifies the peak of a town. No one possibly could have dreamt that the roughly hewn stones supporting the masonry of their crude dwellings would some day become the foundation stones of an architecture second to none and of a story unique in the annals of history.

When the visitor ascens the hill and looks upon the rock beneath the dazzling light of the Grecian sun, he is overawed by the grandeur of the monuments and the richness of its history. Well might he exclaim in astonishment that he has never set eyes on a more glorious stony vision. One can still touch stones whose age goes back to remotest times, those huge boulders of the Cyclopean walls which protected the royal places in the Mycenaean period when kings and retainers had their residences built in a fortified acropolis for security from their foes. The Athenian Acropolis was one of the numerous Mycenaean citadels, though not among the foremost. With the end of the Mycenaean world it would appear that the royal palace was replaced by a structure that was to be known to the Athenians as the "Old Temple" dedicated to Poseidon, got of the spring, and to Athena, goddess of the olive-tree. In addition to these patron deities the Athenians honoured and worshipped in the vicinity of the temple other gods, and demi-gods, heroes and benevolent spirits, and "guardians of the city".

THE ARCHAIC PERIOD

In the early Archaic period, at the close of the 7th and the beginning of the 6th century B.C., in addition to the large "Old Temple" which had been rebuilt, there were erected other temples and sacred buildings. In the age of Peisistratos, when the first Panathenaic festival was celebrated (566 B.C.), the Myceanaean gate in the western entrance and the Mycenaean tower were demolished to be replaced by the first monumental Propylaia and an altar to Athena Nike. During the rule of the Peisistratidai (529-520 B.C.) the "Old Temple" was again reconstructed more sumptuously and adorned with remarkable marble sculptures in the pediments. This was the period when Athens and its art flourished. The worshipper who visited the sacred rock could rightfully gaze with pride on both the Archaic structures with their multi-coloured pediments and the numerous statues, delightful maidens and graceful horsemen set on elegant pedestals in the open air, pious offerings of the faithful and the grateful to the patron goddess who watched over the city, its citizens and its artists.

Towards the end of the Archaic period the Athenians began to build to the south of the "Old Temple" another large temple of Athena, probably on the site of an older edifice. But calamitous events occured soon after the foundations had been laid and the first columns raised. In 480 B.C., after crossing the pass of Thermopylai, the Persian host invaded Athens and put the city and its altars to flames. The Acropolis was not spared. Then followed the naval battle and momentous victory of the Greek fleet at Salamis and the final annihilation of the Persian invaders at Plataiai. The Athenians, who had wisely followed the counsel of Themistokles to abandon the city before the advancing Persians, returned to find nothing but ruins and ashes. The sacred buildings and temples on the Acropolis had been consumed by fire, and the broken statuary lay scattered on the sacred rock. There was neither time, nor the means available to restore immediately the shattered shrines. An ancient tradition has it that following their victory at Plataiai the Greeks had taken a vow to their gods to the effect that they would not touch the destroyed temples but preserve them as eternal reminders of the barbarian invasion. Nevertheless, they gathered with great care and piety all the fragments of despoiled statues and architectural sculptures and buried them on the Acropolis in pits which they covered with soil. Known to the archaeologists as the "Persian deposit" or "layer of Persian destruction", these fragments were found *in situ* by Greek archaeologists when they undertook excavations from 1885-1891 to explore and clear the Acropolis of its debris.

THE CLASSICAL PERIOD

The new generation of Athenians after the Persian Wars built the famous long walls, organized the first Athenian League as a defence against the Persian menace, and laid the foundations of the economic and social structure which was to lead to the city's political and cultural renaissance. Those who had fought in the battles of Marathon and Salamis lived with memories of heroic deeds when their sons assumed the reins of government.

The political history of the fifty years between the defeat of the Persians and the outbreak of the Peloponnesian War (480-430 B.C) is marked by the steady advance of the Athenian democracy to domination of the Greek World and the increasing attraction exercised by the city itself on the rest of Greece. Some of the most creative minds from cities throughout the whole of the Greek World helped to make Athens the great political and intellectual centre it was in the 5th century: architects, sculptors and painters, philosophers and poets all came to the "School of Hellas" and created a world in which the traditions and achievements of every part of Greece were interwoven. The result was that when, at the end of the 5th century B.C., Greek art acquired a uniform language throughout most of the Greek World, this language bore the stamp of the Athens of Perikles and Pheidias. Born in the year of the battle of Marathon (490 B.C.), Perikles, who led the democratic faction and was a friend of Sophokles and Anaxagoras, had grandiose plans for the city. He dreamt of Athens as the leader of a panhellenic confederacy, as an ideal democracy, and above all as a city with magnificent edifices, temples and public buildings, theatres and odeia. Never before or since have so many architectural and artistic works been planned for such a short period of time. The speed with which the majority of them were brought to completion stemmed from the dynamism of the State, and is all the more remarkable in that a large number of them were erected almost simultaneously. The interval between 449 B.C., and

7

the outbreak of the Peloponnesian War in 431 B.C., saw the commencement and completion of work on the Parthenon, the "Thiseion", the Propylaia, the temple of Ares, the temple of Poseidon at Sounion, that of Nenesis at Rhamnous and the temple on the Ilissos. All of this presupposes a carefully worked out "area plan"; some such plan must certainly have existed for the classical monuments on the Acropolis and constituted a major innovation in Greek architecture.

Certainly the most significant and ambitious project of Perikles involved the reconstruction of the Acropolis. With Pheidias as adviser, the plans were soon laid. First and foremost would be a new large temple to Athena Parthenos, the Parthenon, then would follow the monumental entrance to the sacred rock, the Propylaia. Third in order would be the small temple of Athena Nike, the plans of which had already been prepared before the Periklean works. And finally would come the temple to Athena Polias, the Erechtheion. This would replace the "Old Temple", burned down by the Persians, of which only a part of the western section had been subsequently repaired, in order to house the divine wooden image of the goddess — the xoanon "fallen from Zeus" (i.e. from heaven) — which the Athenians had so reverently carried when deserting the city to escape the Persians.

The year 431 B.C., marked the beginning of the Peloponnesian War, the destructive conflict between Sparta and Athens. The building programme of Perikles and Pheidias was not abandoned, however, despite the disasters, death, illness, loss of life and the diminution of Athenian power. Work was resumed in the intervals in the war, and when it finally ended in the crushing defeat inflicted on Athens in 404 B.C., the programme had largely been completed. The Athenian democracy had succeeded in realising one of its finest creations, the complex of buildings on the Acropolis.

The following centuries saw little change in the appearance of the Acropolis, apart from the addition of new dedicatory statues to the many that already existed. The kings of the Hellenistic period deemed it a great honour to have their names recorded amongst the benefactors of Athens, and Antiochos Epiphanes, Attalos II and Eumenes II filled the city with stoas and gymnasia. The stoa of Eumenes dates from the 2nd century B.C. It stood on the south side of the rock and offered shelter from the rain to the audience in the theatre of Dionysos.

The last structure to be erected on the Acropolis was the small circular temple to Rome and Augustus, built before A.D. 14. The square poros foundations of this Ionic monopteral temple still survive.

THE MEDIEVAL AND MODERN PERIODS

In A.D. 267 the city succumbed to the invading Herulii, and was sacked, and it was many years before it recovered. During the following centuries Athens and the Acropolis gradually sank into oblivion and

1. Reconstruction of all the buildings on the Acropolis.

suffered a decisive blow in A.D. 529 when the emperor Justinian closed
the philosophical schools in the city. Despite the survival until the 5th
century of the worship of the Olympian gods, the temples were one by
one converted into Christian churches. This had the effect of preserving
the monuments on the Acropolis, and they survived intact throughout
the Middle Ages. In the Byzantine period the Acropolis became a for-
tress once more; houses were built amongst the ancient monuments and
the 11th century city saw a brief revival of its former glories. After its
destruction by the Saracens in the 12th century, however, Athens was
almost completely deserted. The scholar and metropolitan Michael
Khoniates paints a vivid picture of the distress and desolation prevailing
in the city in the years immediately before its capture by the Frankish
Crusaders.

2. *The Acropolis, the Odeion of Herodes Atticus and the temple of Olympian Zeus in the last century.*

3. The south-west side of the Erechtheion in the last century.

After the fall of Constaninople to the Franks, Athens was acquired by Otto de la Roche, who was given the title *Grand Duke* of Athens. The Catalans, the Acciaioli of Frorence and the Venetians all captured Athens in their turn and converted the Orthodox churches into Catholic. Finally the Turks reached an agreement with the Acciaioli in 1458 and established themselves on the Acropolis; the Parthenon, which had been built as a temple to the ancient gods and had then served the Orthodox and the Catholic churches, ultimately became a mosque.

The monuments on the Acropolis were still in a good state of preservation at this date. The work of destruction began in the 17th century, when the Venetians under Morosini laid siege to the Acropolis. The Parthenon was being used as a munitions store and was therefore bom-

4. The Odeion of Herodes Atticus in the last century.

barded, resulting in an explosion that destroyed a large part of the temple. Further serious damage was caused by the systematic removal of the Parthenon sculptures by Lord Elgin. In 1821, the Acropolis became a battle-field between Greeks and Turks during the Greek War of Independence. On April 25th of that year the inhabitants of Athens and the surrounding area rose in revolt and captured the city from the Turks, the Acropolis falling to them on June 10th after a fierce struggle. After 4 years of freedom, however, Athens was again besieged, on June 28th 1826, by a large Turkish force under Kioutakhis, who captured it in May 1827 and razed it to the ground. The Acropolis capitulated.

Athens finally achieved its freedom on March 31st 1833, when the Turkish garrison handed the Acropolis over to the Greeks. At this date the rock was covered with a motley collection of buildings erected during the Turkish occupation. The task of clearing away the later additions and of collecting together the ancient marbles so that the monuments could be restored and preserved began immediately in 1834. The work lasted for many years but was ultimately successful and occasionally yielded some very striking discoveries. Many of the slabs from the Parthenon frieze which had escaped the eye of Lord Elgin and remained in their native land were found amongst the ruins. They were put on display in the new museum, the foundation for which had been laid in 1864. Work on it was halted immediately, however, when ancient remains were discovered on the site; it recommenced in the following year with new plans, and was finally brought to completion in 1874. It was thus ready when the excavations of Panayotis Kavvadias between 1885-91 revealed the pits in which the remains left after the Persian destruction had been buried; the remarkable archaic sculptures that came to light then are now on exhibition in it.

The Acropolis today faces a threat greater than any in the past: the pollution of th environment. It is to be hoped that the combined efforts of the Greek Government, Unesco, the Greek people and all the friends of the Acropolis through-out the World will be able to preserve the sacred rock once again.

CULT AND MYTH

The Acropolis was not only the hub of the city of Athens, but also the focal point of the entire nexus of mythological beliefs held by the Athenians. All Athenian cults were centered on it, and it was the source of the belief held by the Athenians themselves that they were autochthonous. The name of the city was closely connected with that of its patron goddess Athena, and all the myths explaining the historical origins of the Athenians and their ancient cults are equally inextricably linked with the goddess and the land she chose as her home and over which she extended her protection. A second deity appears as a rival both to Athena and to the mythical forebears of the Athenian: this was Poseidon, who, for all his rivalry, was worshipped not merely alongside Athena, but together with her in the same temple, the Erechtheion, where he was identified with Erechtheus the mythical founder of the Athenian race. The latter was either another name for Erichthonios, or was one of his immediate descendants, and was therefore closely related to the Earth. Thus, from whatever standpoint one approaches the myths and cults of Athens, they lead to the Acropolis and, in the final analysis, to Earth. The view that the cults had their origins in primitive rituals

5. Depiction of Poseidon by the Amasis painter on an Attic amphora of the 6th century B.C. The god has long tresses and beard; he holds a trident in his hand and wears a chiton and a himation. (Paris, Cabinet des Médailles)

dating to the prehistoric period therefore seems well founded. The very fact that all the cults were centred on the area of the Mycenaean palace reinforces the case for their antiquity and their connection with the ancient kingdom of Attica.

It is impossible in a short space to give a comprehensive account of the myths and their relationship to the cults and shrines on the Acropolis. The following brief description merely attempts to trace the threads by which they are interconnected, so as to facilitate an understanding both of the myths themselves and their relation to the centres of worship.

In Attic myth, Kekrops, the founding father of the race and ancestor of all Athenians, was the son of the Attic earth and thus represented a fundamental element of the land itself. The lower half of his body was a serpent, indicating his chthonic origin. During his reign the gods divided up the world amongst themselves and both Athena and Poseidon laid claim to Athens. Poseidon struck the rock of the Acropolis with his trident causing "sea" i.e., salt water, to gush forth while Athena planted an olive tree there in the presence of Kekrops. Zeus then appointed judges to pronounce on their claims. One tradition records that these were Kekrops and Kranaos, the second king of Athens, while another versian claims that the twelve Olympian gods sat in judgement. In any event, the outcome was a vindication of the claims of Athena, who became the patron goddess of Athens. One day, Athena visited the workshop of Hephaistos to ask the god to make her some armour. The same god fell in love with her and, unable to control his passion, attempted to rape her. Despite the attempts of the goddess to defend herself, the sperm of the god fell onto her leg during the course of the struggle, and, in her disgust, she wiped it away with a piece of wool, which she threw to the ground.

The earth was fertilised by the sperm and gave birth to Erichthonios. Athena took the child in her arms and, on the advice of the gods, placed him in a basket which she entrusted to the daughters of Kekrops, Aglauros, Erse and Pandrosos. Overcome by their curiosity they opened it, but were so terrified at what they saw that they threw themselves off the Acropolis in a fit of madness and were killed. One theory was that they saw two serpents in the basket guarding the infant, while another had it that the child had a serpent for a tail, like all the children of Earth. A third version claimed that as soon as the basket was opened, the infant turned into a serpent and glided swiftly to a hiding place behind the shield of Athena, who raised him in her sanctuary on the Acropolis.

6. *Vase painting of Athena of the 5th century* B.C. *The goddess wears the aegis on her breast, and holds a spear in one hand and her helmet in the other. (Musei Vaticani)*

179C

Erichthonios was thus both serpent and man. He became king, married the Nereid Praxithea and sired a son, Pandion. Erechtheus, the son of Pandion and grandson of Erichthonios, was the second great founding father of the Athenians. He had a brother, Boutes, and two sisters, Prokne and Philomela. During the course of a war between the Athenians and the Eleusinians, Erechtheus defeated and slew their king, the Thracian Eumolpos, who was a son of Poseidon. In his anger at the loss of his son, Poseidon sought retribution from Zeus, who destroyed Erechtheus with a thunderbolt.

These and many other myths offer not only an encapsulation of the early history of Athens, but also an explanation of the traditional cults practised by the Athenians on the Acropolis. With the exception of a small area on the north-east of the rock, which was devoted to a sanctuary of Zeus Polieus, and another small section at the south-west end, next to the Propylaia, which was sacred to Brauronian Artemis, the entire Acropolis belonged exclusively to Athena, who was mainly worshipped as Athena Polias, the patron goddess of the city. We may safely assume that the cult of Athena on the Acropolis had very ancient roots and she will undoubtedly have been the most important deity worshipped in the King's palace during the Mycenaean period. This is reflected in Homer when he tells us that Athena entered the "well-built palace of Erectheus".

The earliest preserved remains of a cult building specifically dedicated to Athena are the two stone bases between the Parthenon and the Erechtheion, which are dated to *ca.* 700 B.C. It is also very probable, if not certain, that the 7th century saw the construction of a temple and other cult buildings. Any trace of this earliest phase of the sanctuary, however, has been destroyed by later building activity, and possibly in part by the excavations of the nineteenth century, which went down to bedrock. The history of the buildings on the Acropolis can therefore be traced only from the 6th century B.C., during which one, or possibly two, temples (the forerunners of the Parthenon and the Erechtheion), were built, as well as a large number of smaller cult buildings. It would be pointless to attempt here to describe the remains of all these structures, but it should be emphasized that the sacred areas and the remains of the sanctuaries are all concentrated on the north side of the rock, in the area which was the site of the Mycenaean *megaron* and of the later, 5th century temple of Athena Polias — the famous Erechteion. The official designation of this was "the temple on the Acropolis in which the ancient statue is housed".

The unique form of the Erechtheion was imposed on the architect by the multiple religious and cult purposes it had to serve (cf. the chapter on the Erechtheion). Since it housed so many ancient shrines, it remained the most sacred cult area on the acropolis even after the construction of the most brilliant Doric temple in Greece — the Parthenon, on which the political ambition of Perikles and the artistic genius of

Pheidias stamped the mark of the Athenian democracy. The famous gold and ivory statue of Athena that stood in the *cella* of the Parthenon symbolized the power and confidence of the Periklean state by virtue of the expense lavished on it, and its huge size and superb craftmanship. The wooden *xoanon* of the goddess, "fallen from Zeus", continued to command respect, however; it had been preserved from time immemorial in the "Ancient Temple"; the Erechtheion. And even though it was in the Parthenon frieze that Pheidias portrayed the Panathenaia, the great festival sacred to Athena, the procession in practice ended at the Erechtheion, in which the sacred image of the goddess was housed. According to myth, the festival was first introduced by Erechtheus, and was initially called the "Athenaia," the name being later changed to "Panathenaia" by Theseus, after the unification of Attica. It was reorganised by Peisistratos in the 6th century, after which time the Lesser Panathenaia were celebrated annually, while the Greater Panathenaia were held every four years on the 28th day of the month *Hekatombaion* (July-August). The festivities and the games began on the 21st of *Hekatombaion* and lasted for several days, reaching their climax with the "sacred vigil" on the night of the 27th-28th of that month. Torch races and songs helped prepare the Athenian people for their all night vigil in anticipation of the great day of the sacred procession. The procession itself set out from the Dipylon gate in the Kerameikos headed by an array of State officials, hoplites, cavalrymen and charioteers, followed by the sacred ship, its mast carrying the *peplos* on which was woven a scene of the Gigantomachy, showing Athena struggling with the Giants. Finally came various groups of citizens carrying the offerings and leading the sacrificial victims. The procession advanced through the Agora and up towards the Eleusinion, where it stopped and the *peplos* was taken down, since the slope was too steep for the ship to negotiate. The procession then continued to the Acropolis, passed through the Propylaia and came to a halt first in front of the altar of Athena Hygeia and then in front of that of Athena Polias to the east of the Erechteion, where sacrifices were made to her. Finally the *peplos* was handed over to the priests who "dressed" the *xoanon* of Athena inside the Erechtheion. Part of the famous Parthenon frieze, in which Pheidias immortalized the procession, was until recently in position on the temple, and some of the slabs are on display in the Museum; the majority, however, are in the British Museum in London.

THE MONUMENTS

THE PROPYLAIA

With the completion of the Partehnon, artists and labourers began in 437 B.C. to work on the other monumental structure of the Periklean programme, namely the Propylaia. It was the custom of the ancient Greeks to separate the sacred precincts from the worldly. The entrance to the sanctuaries was usually through a gate or *propylon,* an imposing entrance that prepared the worshipper for entry into the area sacred to the deities before which he would shed all profane thoughts and mundane feelings. We have seen that in the age of Peisistratos a propylon had been built in precisely the same spot where its successor was to stand later. But now Perikles wished to provide the new sanctuaries of the Acropolis with a monumental entrance which would be worthy of the newly built Parthenon and the other temples included in his plan, particularly the building intended to replace the ruined "Old Temple". Iktinos was unavailable for this structure since Perikles had assigned to him the plan for another magnificent building, the Telesterion at Eleusis, where the very ancient and mystic cult of the venerated deities Demeter and Kore was conducted. The Propylaia project was therefore assigned to Mnesikles. Even if nothing else were known about Mnesikles, the Propylaia is sufficient proof that he was a peer of Iktinos in the architectural arts. Never before or since has such a monumental entrance been built, in which grandeur and magnificence were so harmoniously united in the most daring and imaginative archirectural fashion to resolve the nearly insurmountable problems arising from the narrowness of space and the irregularity of the terrain. When in 432 B.C. Pheidias was putting the finishing touches to the sculptural ornamentation of the Parthenon, Mnesikles was completing his equally imposing Propylaia.

The functional and architectural problems posed by the nature of the structure and the configuration of the terrain and space available were enormous. The central section, the *propylon* proper, was given monumental form and flanked by symmetrically arranged buildings. The most important of these was the Pinakotheke on the north wing, an art gallery in which paintings executed on wooden plaques were exhibited. The *propylon* had an outer and an inner facade, both supported by six Doric columns with five doors between them, the largest in the centre. The two colonnades were too far apart to support the roof without the aid of internal supports, and here use was made of Ionic columns; being more slender than Doric, they permitted the optimum usage of the restricted space. The building thus combined the two orders and prepared the visitor for the styles that he would meet on the Acropolis itself (fig. 15, 20, 21).

THE TEMPLE OF ATHENA NIKE

The worship of Athena Nike on the Acropolis was very ancient. To the south of the Propylaia, on the right as one ascends the sacred rock,

7. Reconstruction of the Periclean entrance court of the Acropolis.

there existed an ancient bastion, where an altar was set set up in 566 B.C., the year in which the Great Panathenaic festival was instituted, and a small poros temple was built in the period of the Persian Wars (490-480 B.C.). In 448 B.C. the Athenians decided to erect a new temple to their goddess of victory, designed by Kallikrates. But the execution of the Periklean plan left little room for implementation of the plan until 427 B.C., during the Peloponnesian War, when Kallikrates was finally able to begin the structure which he completed in two or three years, in all probability in 425/4 B.C. The size of the temple was imposed by the confined space, but the architect succeeded in creating a small temple in which architectural grace did not entail the sacrifice of grandeur, and elegance was achieved without the loss of tectonic stability.

It is a small amphiprostyle Ionic temple (fig. 22,23) which rises gracefully on the edge of the rock, where the Athenians worshipped the goddess of victory expressing their hopes for a new triumph in the war

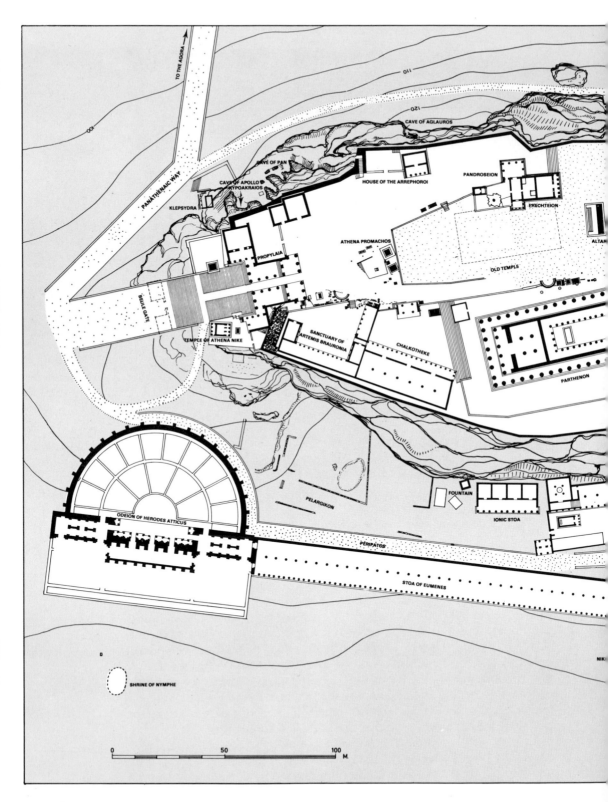

TO THE AGORA

110

120

CAVE OF AGLAUROS

PANATHENAIC WAY

CAVE OF PAN

HOUSE OF THE ARREPHOROI

PANDROSEION

CAVE OF APOLLO
HYPOAKRAIOS

ERECHTEION

KLEPSYDRA

PROPYLAIA

ATHENA PROMACHOS

ALTAR

OLD TEMPLE

TEMPLE OF ATHENA NIKE

BEULE GATE

SANCTUARY OF
ARTEMIS BRAURONIA

CHALKOTHEKE

PARTHENON

ODEION OF HERODES ATTICUS

PELARGIKON

FOUNTAIN

IONIC STOA

PERIPATOS

NIKI

STOA OF EUMENES

SHRINE OF NYMPHE

0   50   100
                              M.

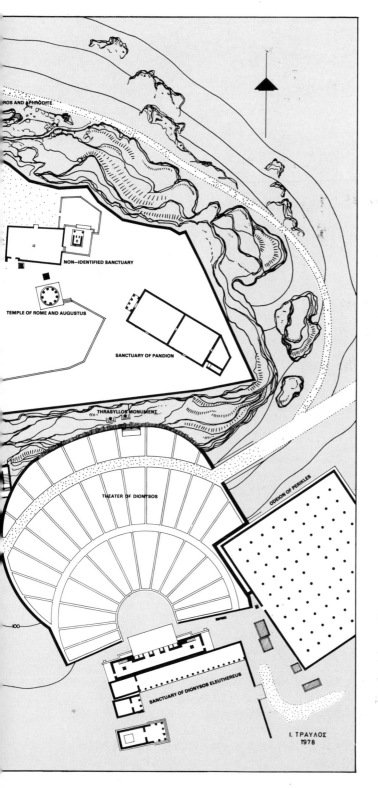

ROS AND APHRODITE

NON—IDENTIFIED SANCTUARY

TEMPLE OF ROME AND AUGUSTUS

SANCTUARY OF PANDION

THRASYLLOS MONUMENT

THEATER OF DIONYSOS

ODEION OF PERIKLES

SANCTUARY OF DIONYSOS ELEUTHEREUS

I. ΤΡΑΥΛΟΣ
1978

PLAN OF THE ACROPOLIS

The drawing shows the buildings on the south side of the Acropolis the peripatos — the path that encircled the rock, and the Panathenaic Way. As well as the four best preserved monuments (the Parthenon, the Erechteion, the Propylaia and the temple of Athena Nike) other buildings that were destroyed over the centuries are also marked — for example the sanctuaries in the area to the south-west. According to J. Travlos there was a courtyard between the Parthenon and the Erechteion known as the sacred court at which the Panathenaic procession ended.

23

8. *Reconstruction of the temple of Athena Nike.*

of those years when they were fighting desperately for victory on land
and sea against the Spartans and their allies. Following the example of
Pheidias' frieze of the Parthenon, the representations on the frieze of the
temple of Athena Nike recalled not a traditional legend of Athens but
the historical battle of Plataiai where the Greeks decisevely defeated the
Persians. When the temple was completed in the turmoil of the Peloponnesian War the Athenians added a protective parapet. The parapet was
composed of marble slabs decorated on the outside with fine reliefs
depicting winged victories with folded or extended wings setting up

trophies or leading sacrificial animals to honour the great goddess who was seated proudly on the rock. It was but an expression of the Athenians' determination and hope for final victory. Those of the slabs that have survived are now in the Acropolis Museum (fig. 77).

THE PARTHENON

The Parthenon is undoubtedly the most magnificent monument of Periklean Athens, and reflects in the sphere of architecture the advanced form of democracy attained by the city. The temple is dedicated to the goddess Athena, who was in a sense the apotheosis of the Athenian state, and the form of the Parthenon as conceived by Perikles and his advisors is fundamentally and indissolubly linked with the goddess and was a magnificent statement of the achievements of the city at the height of its power (fig. 24-30).

The architects of the Parthenon were Iktinos and Kallikrates, and the sculptor Pheidias exercised a general supervision of the work and had a decisive voice in determining the plan of the temple. Iktinos and Pheidias, both experienced artists, were clearly influenced by contemporary intellectual trends, and introduced a number of creative innovations. The temple of Athena Parthenos was a unique and inspired combination of elements from both the Doric and Ionic orders, and the result was a new architectural form which may properly be called Attic. The creation of a work like this demanded vision in its conception and consummate skill in the designing and building of it. It also required the expenditure of enormous sums of money which only Periklean Athens could have met in so short a space of time: for work on the Parthenon began in 447 B.C., and the temple itself was finished nine years later in 438 B.C., though it was a further six years before the pedimental sculptures designed by Pheidias were in position. This achievement is all the more impressive in view of the sheer scale, as well as the quality, of the work. The stylobate measures 30.88 m. x 69.50 m., making the Parthenon the largest Doric temple ever completed anywhere in the Greek world (the temple at Selinous, and that of Zeus at Akragas are the only two largest temples, and neither was ever finished). It is also the only Greek temple built entirely of marble, and the only Doric temple in which all 92 metopes bore relief decoration. The measure of the architectural achievement, however, is to be sought not so much in the statistics of the building as in the exquisite quality of the work, and the artistic inspiration that has transcended the material used in it. For the first time in Greek architecture, the temple ceases to be simply a monument standing within a space and creates its own internal space, which in turn imposed the external form. The demand for internal space apparently derived from the intention of Pheidias to erect a huge, 12 m. high, gold and ivory statue of Athena in the *cella,* consideration that had a decisive effect on the plans. The temple was built on the *krepis* of its predecessor, and use was made of any material that had not been irreparably damaged by the Persians. A number of basic features were retained from the earlier temple: the *pronaos* and *opisthodomos* were prostyle, not *in antis,* and were very shallow; the room at the west end with Ionic colums had also been a feature of the earlier temple; and the length was approximately the same (69.50 m. as compared with the 66.94 m. of the earlier temple). The new temple was much wider, however, (30.88 m. as opposed to 23.53 m.) which posed several problems. The change was clearly dictated by the need for internal space, for the *cella* is 19 m. wide — comparable with those in the enormous temples of Ionia — and occupies approximately 5/7 of the total width of the temple.

This fundamental consideration, however, is incorporated into the general design in such a way that it ceases to be an externally imposed requirement and becomes an integral part of the architectural form. The proportions of the building are governed by a general mathematical principle: the ratio of the width of the stylobate to its length is 4:9, while the diameter of the columns is 1.905 m. and the intercolumniation 4.296 m. — again a ratio of 4:9. The same ratio holds for the height of the temple to its width (13.72 m: 30.88m=4:9), and the width of the temple proper to its length, while the ratio of the width of the temple to its height is 16:81, or $4^2:9^2$.

There are 8 columns along the short sides, which is a number very rarely found; the long sides have 17, however, and conform to the classical principle that they should be one more than double the number on the short sides. To this end, the columns are narrower than usual (ratio of diameter: height=1:4.48) and they are set unusually close together (the intercolumniation is 2.25m. at the bottom; in the case of the temple of Athena Aphaia on Aegina it is 2.65, and for the temple of Zeus at Olympia, 2.32). The slenderness of the columns is reinforced by the lightness of the entablature, which is 3.295 m. high, that is only 1.73 x the diameter of the columns (compared with 1.99 for the temple on Aegina and 1.81 for that at Olympia). The closeness of the columns of the *pteron,* which means that the entire colonnade has to be viewed as a single, indivisible unit, is further emphasised by the narrowness of the porticoes between the *pteron* and the temple proper (their width is less than half the intercolumniation), and by the hexastyle colonnades in front of the *pronaos* and the *opisthodomos,* which create the impression of a dipteral temple like those in Ionia.

The compact and forceful exterior form thus created stands in deliberate contrast to the spaciousness of the interior. The mathematical width of the *cella* noted above (19 m.) was not of itself enough to create this impression of space. It was aided by an imaginative innovation on the part of the architects: the interior double colonnades are connected

10. Colour reconstruction of the north-east side of the pronaos.

by a transverse colonnade at the end of the *cella,* which has the effect of breaking the line of the axis of the central aisle and emphasizing the width. At the same time it established a background on three sides for the gold and ivory statue which stood a few metres in front of the transverse colonnade.

In addition to these brilliantly conceived solutions to the basic architectural problems posed by the building, a series of imperceptible refinements were incorporated into the structure from which the Parthenon derives an inner dynamism. These refinements fall into two categories: the use of curvature and of inclination. The former is observable in the stylobate, the epistyle, the triglyphs, the *geison* and the pediments, and includes the *entasis* of the columns (the thickening that occurs in each column from about 1/3 of the way up). The surface of the stylobate is not perfectly horizontal, as the statics of the building require, but is curved so that the mid-point of the sides is 0.11m. higher than the horizontal, and the mid-point of the ends 0.06 m. higher. The same curvature is applied in the superstructure. Inclination is found in all those elements of the building that should properly be vertical — that is, the columns and walls. The columns of the *pteron* all lean inwards by 0.07 m., and the four corner columns, which form part of two sides, lean diagonally by 0.10 m. The inner surfaces of the walls are vertical, while the outer incline inwards, so that they narrow towards the top. The outer planes of the temple are not parallel, therefore, but converge slightly so that the shape of the building is rather like that of a pyramid, in which there is a movement upwards and inwards.

The brilliance of the artistic conception behind this design is matched by the feat of engineering required to realise it in practice. The differences in the angles and surfaces throughout the building that resulted from the use of curvature and inclination meant that there is not a single stone in the entire structure that is cubic in shape (they are all trapezoidal), and that almost every stone was a different shape and was designed to occupy a unique position. The dimensions of each piece therefore had to be calculated with great accuracy, and the assembly of them required extreme mathematical precision.

The sculptures with which the Parthenon was decorated were in no way inferior to the quality of the architecture. Pheidias had revolutionary ideas and Perikles gave him the means to apply them. Pheidias decided to adorn all 92 metopes of the temple with reliefs, something no Greek city had hitherto dared to attempt, for the cost of such a project would have been prohibitive. The themes selected were derived from the mythical and legendary struggles of Athena and the Athenians: the Gigantomachy — the battle of the Gods against the

11. Colour reconstruction of the gold and ivory statue of Athena which stood in the cella of the Parthenon.

28

12. Reconstruction of the western pediment of the Parthenon depicting the dispute between Athena and Poseidon for the possession of their beloved city. The two deities occupy the centre of the pediment. To the right and left are their chariots and the mythical ancestors of Athens, the families of Kerkops and of Erechtheus.

13. *Reconstruction of the eastern pediment of the Parthenon depicting the birth of Athena who sprang in full armour from the head of Zeus. Right and left of the two main figures, the other gods are arranged in a happy and harmonious assembly. In the two corners are the chariots of Helios, the sun god, and of Selene, the moon goddess.*

Giants in which martial Athena fought bravely — was depicted on the eastern side; the Amazonomachy — the fight of the Athenians led by Theseus against the Amazons who had reached the very hill of the Areopagos — was represented on the western side. The southern side told the story of the Centauromachy — the battle of the Lapiths and their king Peirithoos who with his friend Theseus overcame the terrifying Centaurs. The northern side contained scenes from the Trojan War related to Attic heroes, including the sons of Theseus, Demophon and Akamas, who had joined Agamemnon in the great expedition. The metopes adorned the exterior of the temple and suffered severe damage with the passing of centuries. Most of those that have survived (largely from the southern side) are now exhibited in the British Museum.

The metopes provided Pheidias with ample space to record the age-old myths of Attica and that legendary story of the Gigantomachy showing the triumph of the Olympian gods who first destroyed the primordial Titans, then crushed the Giants, the younger offspring of Ouranos and Gaia, to establish themselves as the almighty deities of the new divine rule and order. This was a grand theme giving any master scope enough to display his talents. Yet it was not enough for Pheidias. With Perikles and other inspired poets and philosophers of their intimate circle, spurred on by the vision of an Athenian democracy at its most creative moment, Pheidias conceived a daring and unique plan: he would immortalize Athens in marble, its people, the youths, the maidens, the men, and their gods, all in a single composition, on the happiest and most celebrated day in their lives when the joyous Athenians, with their hearts beating as one, climbed in procession up the Acropolis to worship their beloved goddess Athena Parthenos amidst all the gods who joined them in the celebration. Pheidias had often seen the splendid procession on the occasion of the Great Panathenaia in the heart of summer towards the end of July (the 28th day of *Hekatombaion*), beneath the brilliant sun of Attica, moving in wave after wave of people behind the sacred vessel upon whose mast hung the *peplos* of Athena, woven by the maidens of Athens to be handed to the priests of the goddess. This vibrant vision, a living image of Athenian democracy, inspired the hearts of its leading men. Perikles praised the glory of Athens in his *Funeral Speech* when he called upon the citizens to be "lovers" of such a unique city whose power and glory were reflected in its remarkable works. (And it is certain that Perikles must have glanced with pride at the Parthenon, which had only then been completed, when he delivered his speech.) Sophokles, too, then an old man of 90 years, sung the praises of the great city with incomparable lyricism in the chorus of the tragedy *Oedipus at Colonos*.

But Pheidias was sculptor; and a hymn is not easily rendered in stone. One had to combine the mind of a genius, the experience of a craftsman and the daring of a pioneer to achieve this feat. To express his vision in marble the space available in the metopes or the pediments of the Doric temple was far too limited. And so he introduced a new element to the Doric edifice by adding a feature that traditionally was part of the Ionic order: a frieze, an uninterrupted zone of marble slabs on which he could carve his vision in relief. A suitable architectural space was needed for this additional feature and the inspired artist unhesitatingly placed the frieze above the temple proper, that is above the architrave of the *pronaos* and the *opisthodomos* and over the side walls of the *sekos*. He thus had at his disposal an area measuring 160 metres in length and 1.06 metres in height. In this space he unfolded the picture of a Panathenaic procession in truly remarkable fashion. Starting out from the southwestern corner the procession moves in two directions: from the end of the western side the horsemen move towards the north, and from the norhwestern edge the procession continues along the north side towards the northeastern end. The other wing of the procession advances along the southern flank from the southwestern to the southeastern end. The two gracefully moving streams of people, the northern and southern, converge at the centre of the eastern side where the gods are seated in divine majesty (for more details see captions to figs. 40-49 and 73-76). The sections of the frieze running along the eastern and western sides of the temple are the most remarkable both in conception and execution. Of these only the western section has survived *in situ*. But its location makes it difficult for the observer to see it at close enough range and appreciate the incomparable perfection of the sculptures. To make up for this and enable the reader to enjoy the Pheidian masterpiece, special emphasis has been given to the subject in this edition. Of the rest of the frieze, several slabs, in fact some of the very best, are now housed in the Acropolis Museum. But by far the greatest number along with what has survived of the pediments are today the pride of the British Museum, which purchased them from Lord Elgin in 1816.

The temple was finally completed in 438 B.C., when the famous gold and ivory statue of Pheidias Athena was set up in the *sekos*. The only portions of the temple not then completed were the sculptures of the pediments. These two vast compositions were the high points in Pheidian art, for they could be more easily enjoyed than any other sculptural work by all the citizens of Athens. Pheidias himself and his most talented assistants Alkamenes and Agoraktitos worked on the figures of the gods and heroes who were represented in the two pediments. On the eastern pediment Pheidias related the birth of Athena who sprang in full armour from the head of Zeus. Zeus was seated in the centre, while on either side the gods were arranged in a happy and harmonious assembly. In the two corners were the chariots of Helios, the sun god, and of Selene, the moon goddess, the former mounting from the ocean, the latter descending into the ocean. The western pediment depicted the dispute between Athena and Poseidon for the possession of their beloved city. Poseidon produced water by striking the rock with his trident and Athena made an olive-tree grow. Athena was judged the winner of this divine contest. The two deities occupied the centre of the pediment. To the right and left were their chariots and the mythical ancestors of the Athenians, the families of Kekrops and of Erechtheus. What had been spared in the passage of countless centuries, by weathering and destruction at the hands of man, was removed by Lord Elgin. These pieces, the priceless survivals of the finest creations of Classical sculpture, are now displayed in special rooms of the British Museum.

THE ERECHTHEION

There can be no doubt that the Periklean plan included plans for the temple which was to shelter the ancient cult statue. The western portion of the "Old Temple" destroyed in the Persian invasion was in all probability restored in order to house the *xoanon* of the goddess and other cult relics. Yet no one, least of all Perikles, could possibly have accepted the sheltering of the most sacred image of the goddess in a temporary and incomplete structure, particularly since she was worshipped there under the name of Athena Polias, patroness of Athens. Another good reason for believing that the sanctuary had been included in the original plan of Perikles is the fact that on the site at which it was eventually built there existed other very ancient relics of the Attic cult, the "divine marks", which would have been probably enclosed during the Archaic period in a *peribolos* north of the "Old Temple". But the Peloponnesian War erupted as soon as the Parthenon and the Propylaia were completed. Not long after this, Perikles died in the epidemic which had raged in Athens. Yet the Athenians did not abandon his plans. With the temporary cessation of hostilities brought about by the peace of Nikias in 421 B.C., work began on the temple of Athena Polias, subsequently known as the Erechtheion (fig. 31). The architect who designed the building is unknown, but one finds it difficult not to recall Mnesikles when gazing upon this remarkably graceful Ionic structure, unique in Greek architecture for its originality of conception and its functional adaptation to accommodate the needs of so many cults. Who but Mnesikles could have given such a daring and original solution to the most difficult problems of an irregular terrain and especially the multiple religious needs of the numerous cults. For the structure would primarily provide for the worship of Athena Polias and at the same time that of Poseidon. Moreover, the sanctuary would hold the graves of Erechtheus with the sacred snake, and of Kekrops, the ancestors of the Athenians, as well as the signs from Poseidon's trident which produced water, the "Erechtheis Sea," a well that contained salt water, and the marks from the thunderbolt of Zeus. The altars of Zeus Hypatos, of Peseidon and Erechtheus, of Hephaistos, of the hero Boutes, of the Thyechoos, and the very ancient *xoanon* of Hermes, all had to be ac-

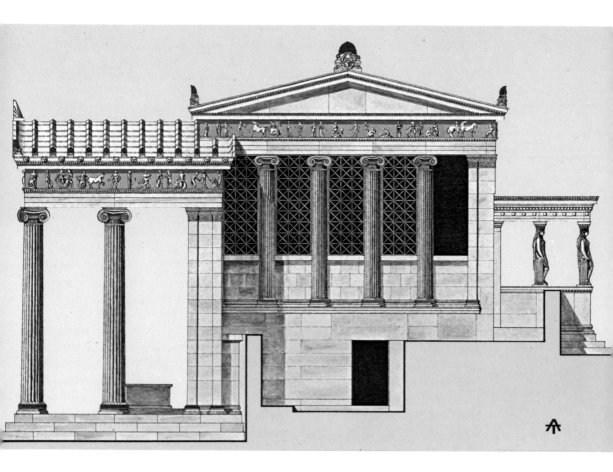

14. Reconstruction of the west side of the Erechtheion.

commodated harmoniously. Lastly room would have to be found for
the sacred olive and the sanctuary of Pandrosos which included the
altar of Zeus Herkeios. The architect succeeded by subtle and ingenious
use of the differences in level to produce an astonishing temple which
satisfied the requirements of all these cults. He respected the traditions
and at the same time introduced striking innovations.

The resulting building may appear complicated at first sight, but it
bears the mark of true genius and contains more original feature than
any other structure in the Greek world. It consists of three almost in-
dependent sections (the main temple, the north extension and the porch
of the Karyatides) with three separate roofs, and is built at four different
levels. Ionic columns of three different dimensions and proportions are
used, and, following an old Ionian custom, use is also made of *Korai* as
supports for the entablature — the famous Karyatides (fig. 32-33). The
temple is divided into two main parts, the east devoted to Athena Polias,
and the west to Poseidon-Erechtheus. The Erechtheion is the finest ex-

pression of the Ionic order, yet the building loses none of the compact austerity of classical Attic architecture. The frieze was of Eleusinian stone of a deep grey colour, and relief figures were attached to it and secured by means of metal connecting pins set in the slabs. Finally, there was a famous gold lamp inside it, made by Kallimakhos, the artist who is traditionally credited with the invention of the Corinthian capital.

SHRINES AND MONUMENTS ON THE SLOPES AND AT THE FOOT OF THE ACROPOLIS

It is the monuments that stood on the summit of the rock and the cults associated with them that account for the importance of the Acropolis in the religious life of ancient Athens and in the history of its art. There were, however, other cult tokens and monuments of considerable importance.

At the west end of the precipitous north side of the rock, below the Pinakotheke, the remains are preserved of the **Klepsydra,** the most important and best known fountain on the Acropolis. Its waters were available to the earliest inhabitants of Athens in the Neolithic period, and it continued in use throughout the whole of antiquity. Close by was the **shrine of Apollo Hypoakraios,** with that of **Olympian Zeus** next to it and the cave of Pan a short distance away. The last was a god much loved by the Athenians, for he had come to their aid at a critical moment during the battle of Marathon. Just beyond the cave, below the north-east corner of the Erechtheion, was the **shrine of Aphrodite and Eros,** not far from which was found an inscription marking the *peripatos* — the path that circled the Acropolis. Two roads leading to the Acropolis ended at this path: the "Panathenaic Way," which started at the Dipylon gate, one of the most imposing entrances in the wall encircling Athens, crossed the Agora and met the *peripatos* at the northwest corner of the rock; and the "Street of the Tripods," which took its name from the tripods dedicated by the victors in the dramatic competitions: this started at the Prytaneion to the north of the Acropolis, skirted the east side of the rock, and ended at the theatre of Dionysos on the south side.

It is the south side of the Acropolis that the visitor first sees, as he walks along Dionysiou Areopagitou street from Hadrian's Arch. If the excavation work had been completed, he would be able to see at his right the foundations of one of the most famous buildings of the Periklean Age, the **Odeion of Perikles,** which stood below the south-east corner of the Acropolis. It was a huge, rectangular building, measuring 62.40 m. × 68.60 m., with internal colonnades, and was the first building in which indoor musical competitions were held. The roof will have been pyramidal in form.

Immediately to the west of the Odeion are the remains of the **theatre of Dionysos,** (fig. 36) in the sanctuary of Dionysos Eleutherios. This was not the theatre in which the earliest plays were produced (until the middle of the 5th century B.C., they were performed in the Agora) but it nonetheless saw the birth and flourishing of Attic tragedy and comedy, and the sanctuary of Dionysos is one of the most sacred places in the history of the human spirit. In its present form the theatre of Dionysos preserves all the marks of its long history, but it is predominantly the theatre created by the *Archon* Phaidros at the beginning of the 5th century A.D. The stone seats which gave the theatre its basic form are earlier, going back to roughly the middle of the 4th century B.C. This was the period of the orator Lykourgos who devised a building programme reminiscent of that of Perikles, which included a monumental theatre in the sanctuary of Dionysos.

The **Asklepieion** was contiguous with the theatre. It was built in the last years of the 5th century when the cult of the healer god came to Athens. The tragedian Sophokles took an active part in the establishment of the new cult. The remains of the sanctuary are today hidden by the foundations of an early Christian basilica dating from the 5th or 6th century A.D., and dedicated to the Ayioi Anargyroi, who succeeded Asklepios in his capacity as god of healing.

The *Peripatos* ran along the south of the Asklepieion and a huge **stoa,** (fig. 37) 161.80 m. long, was built immediately to the south of it in the Hellenistic period by Eumenes II, King of Pergamon (197-159 B.C.). The most impressive structure, the **Odeion of Herodes Atticus** (fig. 38-39) at the north-west corner of the rock, dominates all the other buildings around the Acropolis. Herodes, who lived in the 2nd century A.D., was a lover of philosophy, art and literature and a great admirer of Athens. He used his enormous wealth to bestow generous gifts on the city and to embellish it with great public works, one of the finest of which was his Odeion, built between A.D.161 and 174 in memory of his wife Regilla. The diameter of the *koilon* is 76 m., and it had a seating capacity of 5000. The walls were revetted with marble and it had mosaic floors, a marble floor in the orchestra, seats of white marble and many other expensive features, all of which made it a very imposing building. The most impressive feature was its wooden roof, made of cedar. The ancient sources claim that the audience was impressed e-qually by the techical achievement involved in roofing so large a space and by the artistic elegance of the roof itself. It is today denuded of all these features, and it is only through the testimony of the sources that we can form a proper appreciation of the monument. Fortunately, time has not succeeded in completely destroying the Odeion, and Herodes, the admirer of Athens, continues to make his contribution to the arts in modern Athens, for his Odeion is the largest space available for performances of music and drama.

15. *The Acropolis from the north-west. The Parthenon, Propylaia and the Temple of Athena Nike can be seen. In the background the Panathenaic Stadium is visible.*

16. *General view of the Acropolis and the surrounding area. Lykavittos can be seen in the background.*

17. *The Acropolis from the south-west, with the theatre of Herodes Atticus in the foreground.*

18. *Another view of the sacred rock from the south-east.*

17

19. *The north-west side of the Acropolis, with the temple of Olympian Zeus in the background.*

20. *The north part of the Propylaia. The podium on the left was used as a pedestal for the statue of a four-horse chariot erected by Agrippa.*

21. *The eastern facade of the Propylaia, which had the form of a hexastyle Doric temple.*

22. Part of the entablature of the temple of Athena Nike. The subject chosen for the frieze — the battle at Plataia between the Greeks and the Persians — marked a break with tradition.

23. The small amphiprostyle temple of Athena Nike.

22

24. *The Parthenon, the crowning achievement of Greek architecture, was built between 447 and 432 B.C.*

25. *The east end of the Parthenon. The temple was made unusually wide in order to create an interior space large enough to display Pheidias' masterpiece, the statue of Athena Promachos.*

26. *The Parthenon from the north-east.*

26

27. *The east section of the interior of the Parthenon, from above.*

28. *The north-east corner of the superstructure of the Parthenon.*

29. The north-west corner of the Parthenon.

30. The only part of the frieze stil in situ *can be seen between the columns on the west side of the Parthenon.*

31. *The Erechtheion from the north-west. The architect was constrained by the religious functions of the temple and the uneven surface of the rock to produce a unique building form.*

32. *A view of one of the Karyatides from behind. She holds her head high with a natural grace, and does not seem to feel the weight of the entablature.*

33. *Statues of Korai were used instead of columns to support the entablature in the so-called "Porch of the Karyatides" of the Erechtheion.*

34

35

34-35. *Details of the relief decoration of the proscenium* in *the theatre of Dionysos.*

36. The theatre of Dionysos, on the south side of the Acropolis.

36

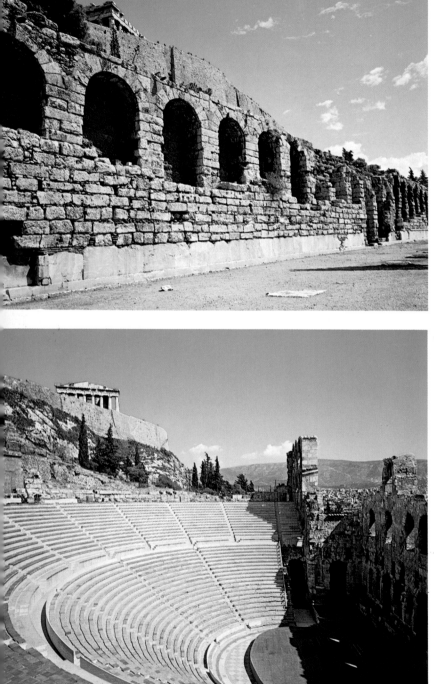

37. The stoa of Eumenes on the south side of the Acropolis.

38. The theatre of Herodes Atticus. It has been restored, and is now again used for performances of drama.

39. The stage of the theatre of Herodes Atticus was decorated with statues and niches and coloured marble.

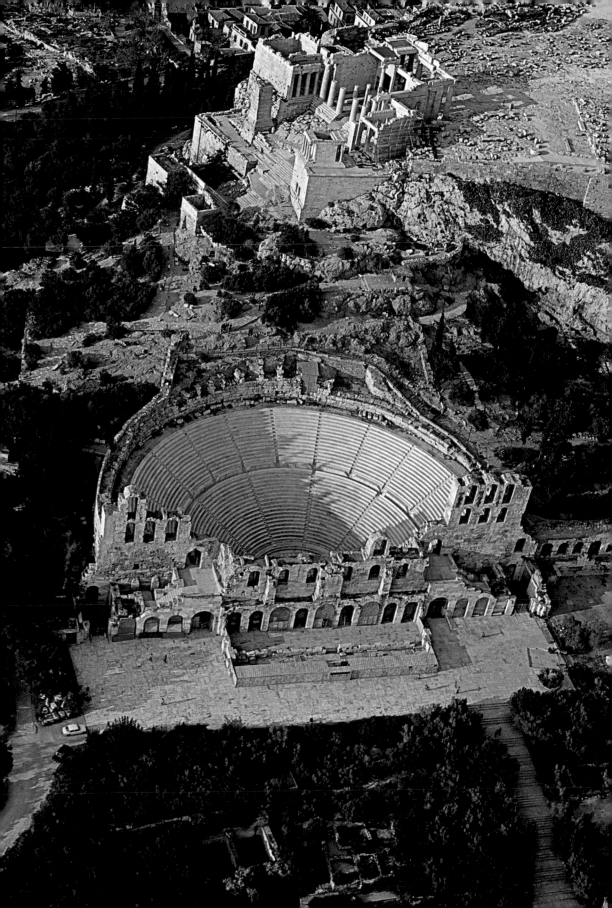

LOBBY

1358. Statue of Prokne
1331. Head of Alexander
1313. Head of a philosopher

ROOM I

1. The pediment of the Lernaian Hydra
4. Lioness devouring a calf
701. Head of a Gorgon

ROOM II

9. Pediment depicting the introduction of Herakles to Olympos
35. The three-bodied monster
36. Herakles and Triton
624. Moschophoros (The Calf-Bearer)
575. Quadriga
593. Kore
4510. Part of the entablature of the "Building C"
4402. Part of the entablature of the temple "A"

ROOM III

3. Pedimental composition: two lions and a bull
632. Sphinx
620. Female figure
619. Kore
618. Kore

ROOM IV

1340. Plaque with the relief of a horse's head
581. Relief of Athena
617. Female (?) head
669. Kore
590. Rampin Horseman
679. "Peplos Kore"
143. Hunting dog
606. Equestrian statue
269. The "Kore of Lyon"
665. Kouros
145. Statuette of "Theseus"
594. Kore
700. Statue of a horseman

673. Kore
629. Statuette of a scribe
675. "Maiden of Chios"
159. Female figure (Nike)
694. Nike
643. Head of a Kore
682. Kore
1342. Plaque with the relief of a charioteer
684. Kore
615. Kore
674. Kore
670. Kore
625. Statue of Athena
595. Kore
685. Kore
680. Kore
671. Kore

ROOM V

681. The "Kore of Antenor"
1360. Kore
691. Small statue of a Nike
683. Kore
631. Pediment of Gigantomachy

ROOM VI

689. The "Blond Youth"
695. Relief of Athena
698. The "Kritios Boy"
686 and 609. The "Kore of Euthydikos"

ROOM VII

885. Torso of Poseidon
881. Torso of Selene (Moon)
1363. Part of a female figure
705. Metope from the south side of the Parthenon
882-884. Fragments of horses from the west pediment of the Parthenon

ROOM VIII

856. Plaque from the east friese of the Parthenon
973. "Nike unlacing her sandal"

ROOM IX

The Karyatides

66

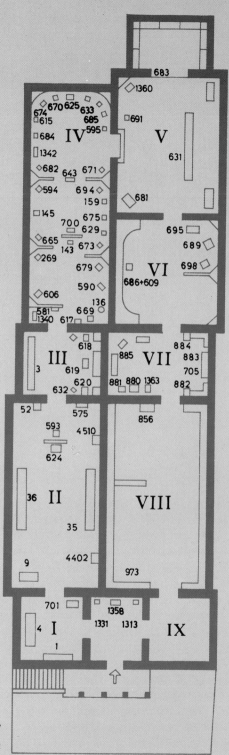

*Plan of the
Acropolis Museum*

67

The Museum

Built as inconspicuously as possible in the southeastern corner of the sacred rock, the Acropolis Museum contains in its few rooms the sculptures found on the Acropolis, votive offerings to Athena or adornments from her temples.

The Museum thus has the finest collection of sculptures and reliefs dating from the culminating period of Greek art. The creations of the Archaic art of the 6th century B.C., collected and displayed in the first rooms of the Museum, and those of the flowering of Classical art which attained its most perfect expression during the thirty of forty years of the second half of the 5th century B.C. in the shape of the sculptures of the Parthenon and the parapet of the temple of Athena Nike, offer the visitor a unique vision of beauty. The purity and intensity of these artistic creations are much enhanced by the manner in which they are presented. Their display to best advantage is due to the painstaking efforts of a scholar of great experience and rare sensitivity — Giannis Miliadis, the Museum Curator in the post-war period. When the Museum was reconstructed, he and his able assistants undertook with great devotion and patience to dismantle nearly all the sculptural pieces, to remove the harmful iron links that held them and to reassemble them as they are seen at present. In certain instances the work involved a major rearrangement of the fragments and Miliadis succeeded in giving us practically new masterpieces, such as the superb Athena from the pediment of the temple of the Peisistratidai.

ARCHAIC SCULPTURES: PEDIMENTAL COMPOSITIONS

The first collection of Archaic sculptures holds one's undivided attention for here are seen the remarkable pedimental sculptures of the early 6th century B.C. The "frightening monsters" with their superhmuman strength and daemonic power, and the poros lions tearing at the flesh of frail calves are the first striking sculptural works to meet the eye. One should visualize them in their deep blue and flaming red colours set in the pediments of a temple bathed by the bright sunlinght of Athens. They now rest in a very confined space with their frightening countenances suggestive of power as it had been skilfully and bodly expressed by the Archaic artists. Their purpose is not to relate a story, but merely to remind on one of the existence in the worlld of terrible powers that are overawing and overwhelming. Such are the "frightening monsters". Yet there is no one more powerful than man. The renowned Herakles fights and overcomes one such terrible monster, Triton, and the "old man of the sea" with his three-bodied dragon-like figure and the three human awaits at the other end of the pediment holding in his human hands a bird — symbol of the air — water and fire (fig. 51). In this characteristic pedimental composition which preserves the colours remarkably well, especially in the faces and the torso of the "three-bodied monster," Attic sculpture displays the terrible power of supernatural beings but at the same time projects the human being, both heroic and mythical, who succeeds in harnessing this power. And it is certainly not a coincidence that among these sculptures in poros stone dating to the early third of the 6th century B.C., in addition to the above-mentioned fight scene between Herakles and Triton, there is a second pedimental group depicting the same theme, and yet a third representing the theme of the Lernaian Hydra (fig. 50), where the artist succeeded for the first time to convey a unity of plasticity, and narrative power. Finally there is a fourth scene depicting the introduction of the hero to Olympos. It should be remembered that the son of Zeus and Alknene did not use his divine powers merely to make a show of his strength. Nearly all his famous labours had a single purpose which one could perhaps describe as philanthropic and cultural. Man's presence and triumph are the subject of the pedimental compositions just described, which date from the early period when Solon first established his constitution and new order of society in Athens.

From the pedimental sculptures, which had belonged to the earlier Archaic temples of the Acropolis until their ruin by the Persians, the visitor moves on to the precious votive offerings that adorned the sacred area before its desecration.

EARLY ARCHAIC VOTIVE OFFERINGS

Sphinxes set on columns, four-horse chariots boldly carved in relief on marble slabs, modest *Korai* and other such dedications were the usual themes in this early period. Yet among these works there were certain masterpieces which now hold a prominent place in the Museum. "Rhombos son of Palos dedicated this" reads the inscription carved in archaic fashion from right to left on the base of the "Calf-Bearer" (fig. 54). One cannot but admire the Athenian artists who in so early a period of their history were able to attain such a flowering of expression. For this superb group of man and animal, dated to *circa* 570 B.C., is an outstanding work of art. The solid sculpture, the well-ballanced figures, and the distribution of weight with the fine positioning of the arms of the man and the legs of the animal in crosswise fashion, are convincing evidence that the anonymous artist must have been an innovator with much experience, unusual sensitivity and rare skill. This work marks the beginning of a remarkably productive period of sculptural art, the likes of which would only be found in the great eras of art history.

A few steps farther, one comes to a second incomparable artistic creation. The name of the artist is unknown, hopefully not forever, for he is represented in this beautiful corner of the Museum in a succession of works. The National Archaeological Museum houses the fine relief of the "Discus-Bearer" which could well be his work. And the Louvre contains another of his works, a head from the Rampin Collection, that has given the artist the name by which he is now known: "sculptor of the Rampin head." In 1935 a torso was identified as belonging to the head and is desplayed at present in the Acropolis Museum. The identification owes much to the scholarly and artistic acumen of the well-known British archaeologist Humfry Payne. Thus one of the finest works of Attic art dating to the mid-6th century B.C., has survived. The work in question is none other than the horseman one can see in the Acropolis Museum (fig. 55) — the head of the statue is a cast made from the original in the Louvre (a cast of his torso has been made for the Louvre head). Next to the horseman is the famous "Peplos Kore" and beyond that the hunting dog and the lion's head, all evidence of what this great artist was able to create in the twenty or thirty years of his career.

THE ARCHAIC KORAI

The statue of the "Peplos Kore" is remarkable for its structure: the firmly shaped lower part of the body, the sensitively modelled breast, covered by a double fold of the dress (the curve of the fold, which follows the movement of the figure, is exquisite) and discreetly framed by the fine locks of her hair. The attractive young head has features that are vivid and at the same time soft and gentle (fig. 59). It is extraordinary how the artist has succeeded in conveying so much humanity, nobility and feminine grace in so delicate a figure of a young maiden and at the same time to make her so intimately familiar, yet unearthly and divine. She regards one with complacency and dignity, with an imposing air, as she becomes the symbol of a fully developed artistic and spiritual expression. The next exhibit, the hound with its tensed muscles ready to punce forward, holds the eye and compels the visitor to linger a while longer in this magnificent corner of the Museum. But so many other Korai await, so many graceful maidens dressed in fine Ionic *chitons* and rich *himatia,* decked with earrings, their hair adorned with diadems, a smile on their lips, standing in a circle as though ready to begin a dance.

Broad-chested, robust, and imposing, the firm figure of the representative Athenian maiden stands before the visitor (fig. 57). This is a dedication by the potter Nearchos to the patron goddess of the city. The donor must have been both a wealthy and a pious man to commission Antenor to carve this statue. Antenor was the artist whom the Athenians would ask a few years later to make the splendid group of the Tyrannicides. The dignity of the Kore is more impressive than her grace, since the sculptor emphasized the severe vertical and horizontal lines, diminishing the oblique and diagonal movements characteristic of the Korai of that period (525-500 B.C.).

The height of the small head (No. 643) measures a mere 14 centimetres (fig. 62). It should date a few years later than her bigger sister, the Kore of Antenor, yet how remarkably different is her attitude and expression. It is doubtful whether in the entire production of Archaic art — or for that matter of any art — there is another figure so attractive, so refined and so spiritualized. The dominance of the flowing curve, of eternal movement, conveys an almost ethereal impression. The young flower that has just blossomed and is vibrant with life may be likened to this exquisite face glowing under an imperceptible vibration of the soft skin.

Perhaps for the first time in the history of sculpture the female body had found its fullest expression in the Kore with the "almond eyes" (No. 674, figs. 64 and 67). She is no longer the young maiden with the broad and raised shoulders, the robust woman of Antenor.Here the shoulders, narrow and gently curving, support a long fine neck, sensitively modelled. Without being a frail creature, she is nonetheless so refined, fragile and delicate, that the visitor is immediately drawn to her with a feeling of tenderness. Her face, reflactive, reserved, and at the same time full of radiant confidence, rouses both respect and admiration, in addition to a subtle attraction. The visitor gazes at a maiden of unique personality and perhaps it would not be exaggerated to regard this statue as a brilliant Archaic portrait.

The last Kore on display stands as a landmark dividing the receding Archaic age from the emerging Pre-Classical period. She had been dedicated by Euthydikos (fig. 65). For the first time one sees in this maiden a perfected carving of the body. The artist reveals even the finer details beneath the dress.

This is very evident especially in the back where one can distinguish the furrow of the vertebral column beneath the abundant hair falling over the shoulders. The head with the simple hair — do is a distinctly new element. The delightful expression with the happy interplay of the facial features has been now replaced by an unusual severity that almost suggest melancholy. It reflects the spirit of the early years of the 5th century B.C., of the generation of the warriors of Marathon and the tragic events of the Persian Wars.

The horsemen, brothers of the Korai, accompanied the maidens in the sacred Panathenaic procession. Descendants of the "Rampin Horseman," and forerunners of the riders in the frieze of the Parthenon, the devout Athenians dedicated their images in marble to their beloved goddess. A quick glance at the few superb horses that survive from the final Archaic period reveals the Athenians fondness of this noble animal, but even more so, the unsurpassed talent of Athenian sculptors in creating its likeness in such memorable marble masterpieces (fig. 68).

THE PEDIMENT OF THE TEMPLE OF THE PEISISTRATIDAI

All this statuary was created to please Athena, daughter of Zeus, the great goddess, who had joined her father in the forefront of the terrible war between the Gods and the Giants. In about 525 B.C., the Athenians rebuilt the "Old Temple," predecessor of the Erechtheion. For the first time, during the rule of the Peisistratidai, the entablature and pediments were made of marble. And for the first time on the Acropolis the eastern pediment related the battle with the Giants. There is no doubt that the entire work was put in the hands of a master sculptor. The fragments which have survived from the pediment show that this was the most striking composition of the Archaic period. The Athena and the Giants preserved, particularly the two figures from the extremities of the pediment, reflect the fullest and highest flowering of Attic sculpture. The goddess, who has been restored, has acquired a superb firmness and forcefulness (fig. 58). The sharp lines of the shoulder and legs, the vigorous thrust by the left arm of the *aegis* with the serpents, and the tension in her right arm as she grasps the spear, express in the most effective manner both the divine rage and self-assurance of the martial goddess. These fragments give one a clear idea of how the Athenian sculptors could conceive and transfer into marble the vigorous movements and feelings in the closing years of the Archaic period, and permit one to visualize Antenor's group of the Tyrannicides, which was carried off as a war trophy by the Persian invaders when they left Athens. It would not be strange to presume that the master sculptor who gave Athenian democracy its first official monument was the same person who a few years earlier had carved the splendid pediment which holds one's attention in the last room of the Archaic section of the Museum.

FROM ARCHAIC TO CLASSICAL ART

Now the visitor moves beyond the limits of Archaic art and stands before the first outstanding specimen of the sculpture of the severe style. The National Archaeological Museum houses the last Kouros of Attica, the statue of Aristodikos, wherein had been exhausted all features of the archaic modelling of the male figure. We have strong reason to believe that the youthful figure seen here is a creation of the great Attic artist Kritios. The sculptor has freed himself from the confines of the Archaic past and has created a new balance in the stance of the body (fig. 71). The weight is no longer distributed evenly between the two legs. One is bent slightly at the knee, leaving the support fall fully on the other limb. The poised leg transforms entirely the overall image and the structure of the body, gracing it with a *contraposto* movement.One cannot exaggerate the significance of this striking breakthrough in Greek art, which was to become the heritage of European art. For it is not an external technical solution to the problem of posture. It is in fact a deeper inner refinement and transformation conveying to the figures a new rhythm, replete with spiritual depth. This same style would have been applied to the "Blond Youth" of which only the head survives (figs. 69-70). Divine and attractive in its severe expression, it is simple and firm in conception and reflects an inner vision.

THE PARTHENON SCULPTURES

The "Kritios Boy" and the "Blond Youth" lie between Archaic strength and Classical balance preparing the visitor for the next rooms which contain the sculptures of the Parthenon. Few in number and badly mutilated are the figures that have survived from the pedimental compositions.Most of them had been removed by Lord Elgin to London together with the largest part of the frieze and numerous metopes. No matter how sufficient they are, even in their present state of preservation, to convey some idea of the magnificence of the original composition, they do not hold the visitor's attention long. It is preferable to move on to the fragments of the frieze that have survived in their place of origin.

In this inspiring creation of Classical sculpture, which reveals an unparalleled vision of Athenian glory, divinities and humans acquire a familiarity yet retain a superhuman form. The uniformity of the figures represented subjects them to the polyphonic harmony of the whole without in any way depriving them of their self-sufficiency as individual entities. This creation can and should be enjoyed only as a unified and indivisible whole. Within this unity the horseman is still as noble as is his steed — the presence of man and the animals led to sacrifice cannot be evaluated by different standards. The young and the old, maidens and youths, deities and humans, are all carefully balanced and placed so effectively that they become irreplaceable. Each part fulfils a particular function in the artistic whole so that it becomes impossible to separate and speak of one specific part only. For not only the figures of humans and beasts but also the garments (indeed with what power!), the flying mantles and flowing robes, and even the empty spaces within the reliefs, have their particular reason for being where they are and contribute their share to the easthetic whole.

Bearing this in mind, we shall pause for a moment before the three figures of Poseidon, Apollo and Artemis, from the eastern section of the frieze (fig. 75). The figures of the deities are carved on the same slabs and with the same dimensions as the remaining figures of the frieze. Yet even though limited by the height of the frieze measuring but one metre, these figures manage to assume such an imposing grandeur and stature as to reflect unmistakebly their divine nature. The relaxed posture on the throne, the measured but free movement, the firm bodies of the male divinities, the folds of the *himatia* with their marked regality, next to Artemis, many-pleated *chiton* with its delicate harmony, all set in the ample unencumbered space carrying a striking perception of depth, transport the observer to the serene and lofty abode of Olympos.

Among the outstanding sections of the remaining frieze are the marble slabs carved in relief with the figures of youthful horsemen who convey lively movement to the great Panathenaic procession. Pheidias, creator of the Parthenon, friend and advicer to Perikles, drew from the noisy and tumultous picture of reality the splendid figures that one now sees in a vivid yet disciplined style, rich but concise, both festive and sober. These figures of youths and horses so full of life, with their robust and vibrating strength, have harnessed in artistic manner the movement and the power of the natural being and have attained the highest point of the art of sculpture as they stand forever on "the razor's edge". Along the path to art and artistic expession they reached that height which lasted but a few brief years when the struggle between the spirit and matter was finally resolved by the unique blending never again to be repeated, between the two components of life, alloting to each its rightful and equal share. This brilliant moment found in 5th century B.C.

Athens the man who created artistic perfection in the harmonious features of the Parthenon.

THE SCULPTURES FROM THE PARAPET OF THE TEMPLE OF ATHENA NIKE

In the next moment art began to be transformed. Those who had worked with Pheidias — and perhaps one can distinguish their individual work in certain figures of the Parthenon — charted a new path. They became intrigued by one or another discovery which they now wished to apply in their works. The slabs from the parapet surrounding the bastion where the elegant temple of Athena Nike stands, are displayed opposite the marble slabs of the frieze in the same room of the Museum. They date a few decades later, yet one observes that the Classical moment is beginning to give way to a new vision. The exquisite female figures open or fold their wings surrendering to their rich wavy draperies and to the vigour of their varied movements with multiple artistic results. They rejoice in their suppleness (as when Nike unlaces her sandal, fig. 77) or twist gracefully to create a flying movement of their robes (as when they strive to tame their rebellious victim). Here one still breathes the air of the Parthenon. But the new currents are now considerably stronger and one can foresee fresh forces that will develop to lead to a new era of Greek art.

A few other beautiful examples of Greek art may be seen before departing from the Museum. The Prokne of Alkamenes, one of the marble tiles of the Parthenon, a fragmented relief, an excellent portrait of later antiquity. Yet it would be perhaps wiser if the visitor were to leave this sacred site with the image of the sculptures of the unique Classical moment.

44

40-49. The frieze of the Parthenon is the most striking innovation in the temple. Although the artist was bound by tradition, his genius introduced a daringly new element to temple construction: to the Doric edifice he added a sculptured frieze, i.e. an Ionic element, without in any way destroying the basic Doric structure. The frïeze rested on the side walls of the sekos and above the pronaos and the opisthodomos. Henceforward this innovation was to become a traditional feature. But the fruitful imagination of Pheidias did not restrict itself to this novelty alone. The theme he selected for the frieze was indeed a radical one. He would not, as tradition required, relate the standard myths normally seen in sacred edifices. Next to the age-old myths venerated by the Athenians, Pheidias — a friend of Perikles and Anaxagoras — believed that the legend of the new Athenian democracy should and could be recorded on marble. The city's crowning achievement in peace, an achievement of no less importance than glorious military feats in war, was carved in relief in the grandiose composition of the Panathenaic procession. The Panathenaia was the greatest festival celebrated by the Athenians in honour of Athena, their patron goddess. The festival was held annually, but every four years it assumed a special magnificence, and was hence known as the Great Panathenaia. The wooden xoanon of the goddess, the one believed to have fallen from heaven, was removed from the "Old Temple" (the Erechtheion) and dressed with a new peplos woven in a traditional design. The peplos, spread as the sail of a trireme, was carried from the Kerameikos to the Acropolis in a grand procession. It was this most sacred and splendid procession that Pheidias aspired to immortalize on the frieze of the Parthenon. The frieze itself is a poetic composition in marble which illustrates

and glorifies the holy procession through the art of sculpture. The elements of time and space disappear and all the figures move within an artistic dimension where both mortals and gods coexist harmoniously. The whole composition of the frieze conveys to us the festive spirit of the procession and at the same time transports us ecstatically into the realms of great art. To bring this vision to life the great sculptor resorted to methods that were simple and persuasive. Only a genius could possibly have found the solution to the many problems, the most critical of which was to find suitable points for the beginning and the end of the procession. Moreover he had to select the most characteristic elements that would lend themselves to plastic rendering and to the rhythmic arrangement of the seemingly endless flow of figures. The final solution adopted by Pheidias breathed life into the procession and transformed it into a symphonic unity, in the musical sense, in which were orchestrated all the available elements of reality, art and religion. Thus the entire composition culminates on the façade of the temple at the eastern side where the procession terminates. In the very centre of the eastern side, a male figure (possibly a priest) is depicted receiving the sacred peplos, while two maidens carrying seats are facing a priestess. To either side of this central scene the Olympian deities are seated in relaxed positions, in groups: Zeus, Hera and Iris (?) to the left. Athena and Hephaistos to the right. Next to Hera are Ares, Demeter, Dionysos, and Hermes. Next to Hephaistos is the slab containing the figures of Poseidon, Apollo, and Artemis (fig. 75). The brilliantly calculated placement of this sculptured group above the entrance to the temple in the middle of the eastern side determines the basic arrangement of the remainder of the frieze. For the procession to terminate at this

point, two separate streams of figures were required on the two long sides of the temple moving towards and culminating in the eastern façade. In fact, this was Pheidias' own plan; but had the double procession been divided into two equal parts, the starting point would have to be in the centre of the western side, and at that point there would have been two groups, moving in opposite directions, the one towards the left and the other towards the right. Such a solution was unacceptable to Pheidias. Hence with great ingenuity he selected as starting point the southwest corner, the only point at which the continuity of the moving procession would not be broken. Thus the procession begins at the south end of the western side and moves to the north. In the first slabs, the youths have not as yet mounted their horses, but are preparing to do so. In this way Pheidias appears to be following the ceremony from its very beginning, both in place and time, but in fact he is making good use of this element to open his symphony on a plain low-key (pianissimo). In the sixth slab (figs. 40-43) the first two riders appear and the rhythm becomes more dynamic, yet always retains a subdued tone, as the figures move along at comfortable distances from each other, with two figures at the most in each slab (figs. 45-47). At about the centre is situated the most magnificent relief in which a horse rears wildly on its hind legs and neighs, while a man strives to control it (fig. 44). Then the procession of mounted horsemen moves on somewhat hesitantly (figures on foot are interspersed between the horses). The stream of figures continues along the northern side. The first slab at the western end is like a new, brief introductory scene. The young men still on foot make final arrangements to mount their horses. It is from this point onward that the noble and joyful riders become more

47   *numerous and move impetuously but rhythmically forward (a real allegro maestoso). In these*
reliefs art attains the absolute limits of perfection, for with only the slightest depth there emerge
in crystal-clear purity six and at times seven mounted men, one placed behind the other in suc-
cessive planes. Ahead of the horsemen come the four-horse chariots with their charioteers and
the heavily armed apobatai. *After the closely packed horsemen, this section retains to a certain*
degree the rapid rtythm of movement with the galloping horses, but with a greater spacing out
of the figures it creates a broader and more easily flowing wave preparing as it were for the
move to the groups of figures that lie ahead. These latter slow down the pace of the procession
to a walking gait. First there is a stationary group of older men, then we see the lyre-and flute-
players moving ahead, then follow the hydria-and skaphe-bearers and finally come those who
lead the sheep and oxen to sacrifice. In the second section of the procession that begins at the
west end of the south side, the arrangement of the groups is the same as on the north side. As
has been pointed out, the two streams of the procession converge at the eastern side. From the
two ends come maidens carrying phialai and oinochoai for the libations, and censers, while
others come empty-handed: they are the ergastinai, *the maidens who had woven the sacred*
peplos. Between these maidens and the two groups of gods there is a group of six men on the
left (towards Hermes) and another of four on the right (towards Aphrodite), possibly
representing archons or mythical heroes. The greatest part of the frieze is in the British
Museum. The entire western side is still on the monument; several slabs from the northern, a
few from the southern and two from the eastern sides are in the Acropolis Museum.

83

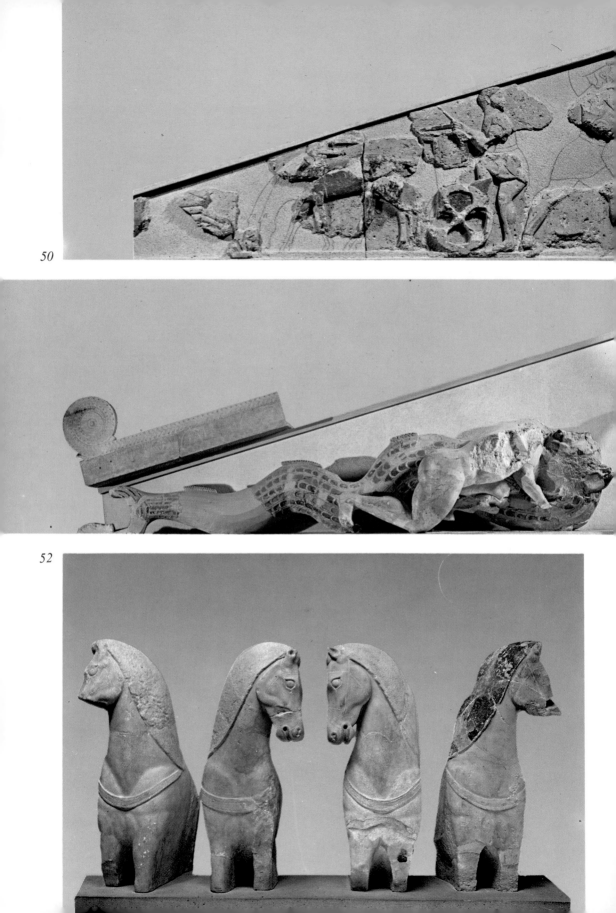

50

52

51

53

50. Poros pediment from an unidentified small building of the early 6th century B.C. Herakles is depicted overcoming the Lermaian Hydra. To the left on the chariot is Herakles' friend Iolaos and in the corner is the Hydra's ally, the "crab".

51. Large poros pediment of the Archaic temple of Athena. On the left Herakles fights against Triton. To the right the "Three-headed Daemon". c. 570 B.C.

52. The four horses come from a marble votive relief. The slab probably carried the representation of a fourhorse chariot and the charioteer. c. 570 B.C.

53. Archaic marble Sphinx. It was set up on a tall column. c. 560-550 B.C.

54

54. The "Calf-Bearer" was one of the earliest compositions of large sculpture in the Archaic period. Rhombos, the man who dedicated this offering, carries on his shoulders the calf he intends to sacrifice to Athena Pallas. An excellent Attic work dating in c. 570 B.C.

55. Shortly before the middle of the 6th century B.C. a splendid monument was erected on the Acropolis, depicting two young horsemen crowned with oak leaves, a symbol of victory. One of the horsemen has survived in a fairly good state of preservation (the head in the Acropolis Museum is a cast of the original head now displayed in the Louvre). It is the oldest statue of a mounted rider in Greek art and the work of a great sculptor of the Archaic period whose name is unknown.

56. It is quite possible that the same artist produced this remarkable hound with its highly tensed body, its sharp planes and the crystal-clear outline capturing in exquisite artistic fashion the spirit of the noble beast. c. 530 B.C.

55

56

57. The "Kore of Antenor". From an inscription on base on which this statue probably stood, we learn that it was dedicated to Athena by the potter Nearchos and was executed by the celebrated Athenian sculptor Antenor who made the first group of the Tyrannicides. The "Kore of Antenor" possesses the dignity and maturity of monumental art. Fashioned with perfect architectural balance, she raises her imposing figure, supported on strictly vertical axes. In contrast with her graceful sisters, she presents a severe structure that was to influence Athenian sculpture in subsequent years. c. 525 B.C.

58. The figure of Athena from the Gigantomachy depicted on the pediment of the temple of the Peisistratidai (c. 525 B.C.). One of the most daring works, it stands as a forerunner of the Attic sculpture of the later Archaic period, and opens new ways to architectural sculptures. It is certainly the work of a great artist of that age — the suggestion that it may well be a work of Antenor seems quite plausible.

59. The "Peplos Kore" is a work of the artist who created the "Rampin Horseman". c. 530 B.C.

60. A later Kore of great artistic sensitivity. She is the only maiden not lifting her himation. c. 500 B.C.

61. One of the most charming of Korai is the so-called "Maiden of Chios", presumably made in a workshop of that island. It retains in excellent condition the colouring of the garments. c. 510 B.C.

62. This small head of a Kore is a real masterpiece of Greek sculpture. The uninterrupted flow of planes gives it a unique attraction. c. 510 B.C.

61   62

63. *This delightful Kore wears only a chiton (the others wear also a himation). The statue is wholly preserved and presents an unusual variation of the Kore type. c. 510 B.C.*

64. *The most attractive Kore of the Athenian Acropolis. In no other statue has the essence of youthful feminine grace been conveyed with such expressive force. The imperceptible curves in the folds of her himation, the refined locks of hair and the superb partition of the hair over the forehead, the full lips, and the enigmatic expression of the eyes, make up an incomparable composition that must have been a harmony in colour in its original state. c. 500 B.C.*

65. *The "Kore of Euthydikos". The inscription on the base records that the statue was "Dedicated by Euthydikos son of Thaliarchos." In contrast to the previous Korai with the Archaic smile, she possesses a severity of expression. The facial features are more simple and austere, the body fuller and riper. These elements suggest a new attitude to life and art that foreshadows the works of the severe style. c. 490 B.C.*

65

66. *Votive relief. Three female figures with fine chitons hold hands and dance, while Hermes plays a double-flute before them. The last female figure holds by the hand a child that has lost the step in its endeavour to follow the dance. Some archaeologists believe this to be a representation of the Aglaurides with Erichthonios as a child. The background of the relief was painted blue. A charming work probably of some island school. c. 500 B.C.*

67. *The attractive head of the Kore no. 674. Archaeologists have named her "the Kore with the pensive face", or "the Kore with the almond eyes". The vibrating surface of the flesh, the triangular forehead framed with the fine arrangement of wavy and flowing hair, the varied colours of the chiton and the harmonious folds of the himation are indeed remarkable.*

66

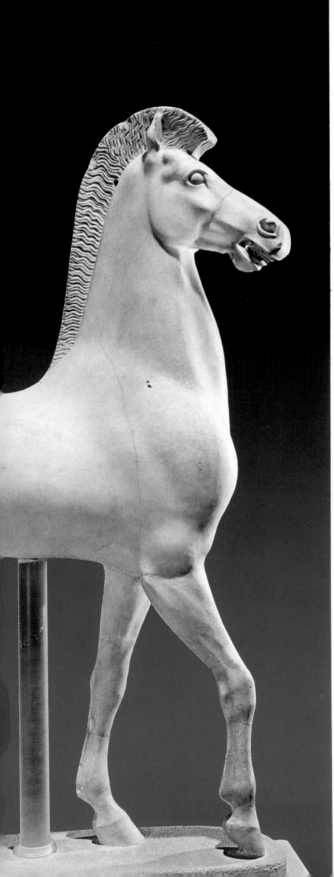

68. *The fore part of a superb horse. The artist conveys with ingenuity and fondness the pride and nobility of the animal that was so admired by the Greeks. c. 490-480 B.C.*

69-70. *Head of a boy known as "the Blond Youth" because when first found a deep yellow tint was still discernible in the hair. The severe expression of his face and the fullness of his flesh are reminiscent of the "Kore of Euthydikos" and indicate the new tendencies in the sculpture of the early 5th century B.C. Judging by the inclination of the head towards the right shoulder, we may conclude that his posture was similar to that*

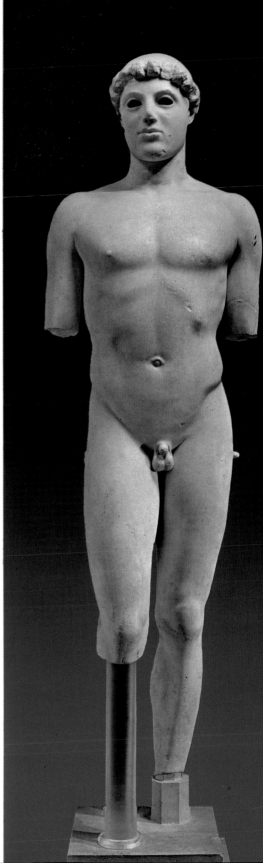

of the youth pictured next to him. Short-
ly before 480 B.C.

71. The well-known "Kritios Boy," so
called because many archaeologists
believe it to be a work of the sculptor
Kritios. This work marks a decisive
break from the Kouros tradition and
opens the way to Classical art through
the slight bend in the right knee. This ap-
parently minor innovation had in-
calculable results. The human body was
liberated creating successive movement
and counter-movement which enabled
the artist to use hitherto unknown
techniques of expression and stance. c.
485 B.C.

70

72. The so-called "Mourning Athena". The goddess wears a helmet and a folded peplos, girded at the waist. Leaning on her spear with the left hand, her body slightly inclined forward, she bends her head and contemplates the stele standing before her. This latter may have been a stele marking out the boundaries of the sacred precinct of the goddess. A superb example of the severe style. c. 460 B.C.

73. Slab from the north side of the Parthenon frieze representing three youths leading two oxen. The rhythmic alternation between the upright youthful figures, dressed in long himatia appropriate to the religious occasion, and the horizontal bodies of the animals results in a composition of counterpoints of a hitherto unmatched harmony and architectural solidity.

74. Slab from the north side of the Parthenon frieze representing six thalophoroi (men carrying olive-branches, which were painted on the slab). They all wear long himatia falling over the left shoulder, exposing their chests.

73

74

75

76

75. One of the finest slabs of the eastern side, in all probability executed by Alkamenes, pupil and collaborator of Pheidias. It represents Poseidon, Apollo and Artemis. Seated in dignity in a relaxed posture they manage to assume greater stature in contrast with the mortals in the procession. Their divinity and majesty are enhanced by the wide space that separates them and the spaces beneath the thrones, conveying at once the feeling that we are now in a different realm from that of the earthly procession in the remainder of the frieze. The relief is of outstanding workmanship.

76. Relief with three "hydria-bearers": a fourth at the right end has bent over to lift his pitcher. The triple repetition of similar forms with only a very slight variation between them and the equal spaces separating the figures, the contrasting folds of their himatia that acquire an even greater intensity as they are accompanied by the plain surfaces of the hydriai, make up a unique ensemble that is but another harmonic theme blending in with the entire composition of the Parthenon.

103

77

77. *"Nike unlacing her sandal." This exquisite figure from the parapet of the Temple of Nike expresses the new trends of Attic sculpture at the close of the 5th century* B.C. *The graceful movement of Nike produces the rich and refined draperies of her chiton and himation.*

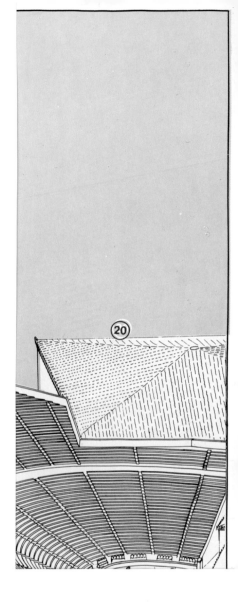